ONDORI
Creative
Gift Packaging

Designed by Yoko Kondo

D1318419

CONTENTS

COLORED PICTURES

BASICS IN MAKING GIFT BOXES

INSTRUCTIONS 36.——89.

★Copyright ©1986 ONDORISHA PUBLISHERS.,LTD. All rights reserved.
★Published by ONDORISHA PUBLISHERS, LTD., 11-11 Nishigoken-cho, Shinjuku-ku, Tokyo 162
★Sole Overseas Distributor : Japan Publications Trading Co., Ltd.
 P.O. Box 5030 Tokyo International, Tokyo, Japan.
★Distributed in the United States by Kodansha America Inc.
 114 Fifth Avenue, New York, NY10011, U.S.A.
 in British Isles & European Continent by Premier Book Marketing Ltd.,
 1 Gower Street, London WC1E 6HA
 in Australia by Bookwise International
 54 Crittenden Road, Findon, South Australia 5023, Australia.

10 9 8

ISBN 0-87040-732-5
Printed in Japan

Various Envelopes

Chopstick Rests

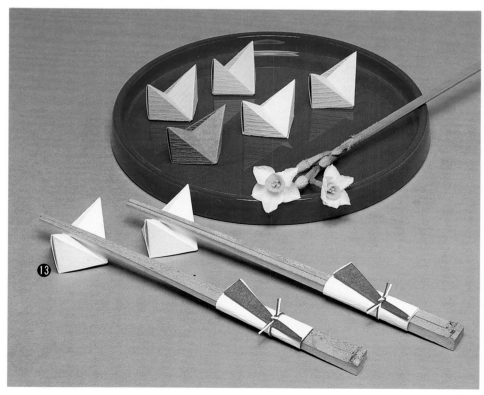

For St. Valentine's Day

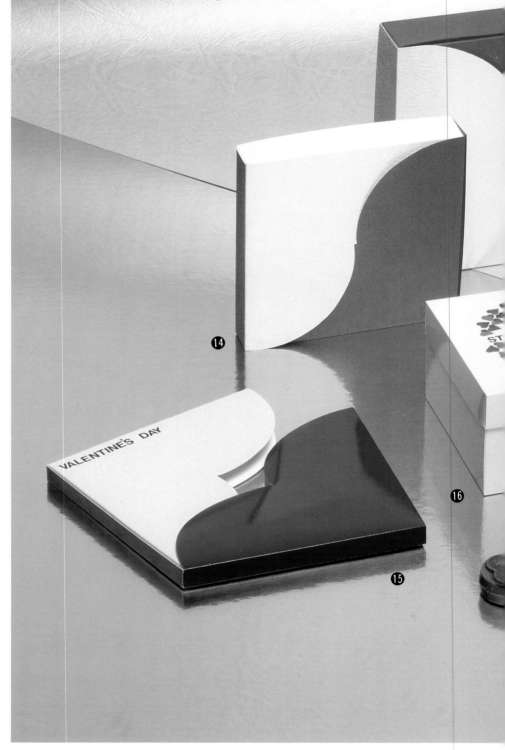

VALENTINE'S DAY

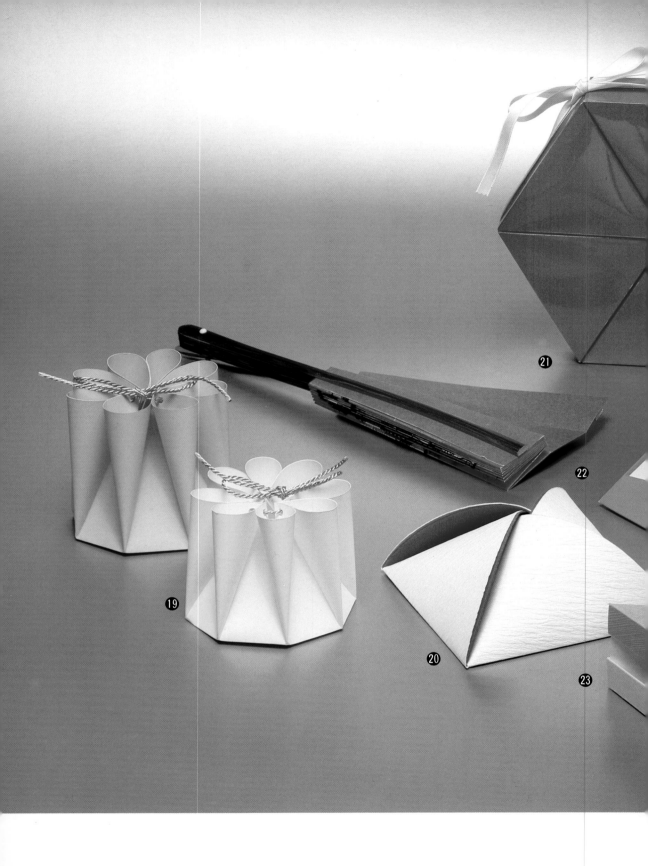

For Girls

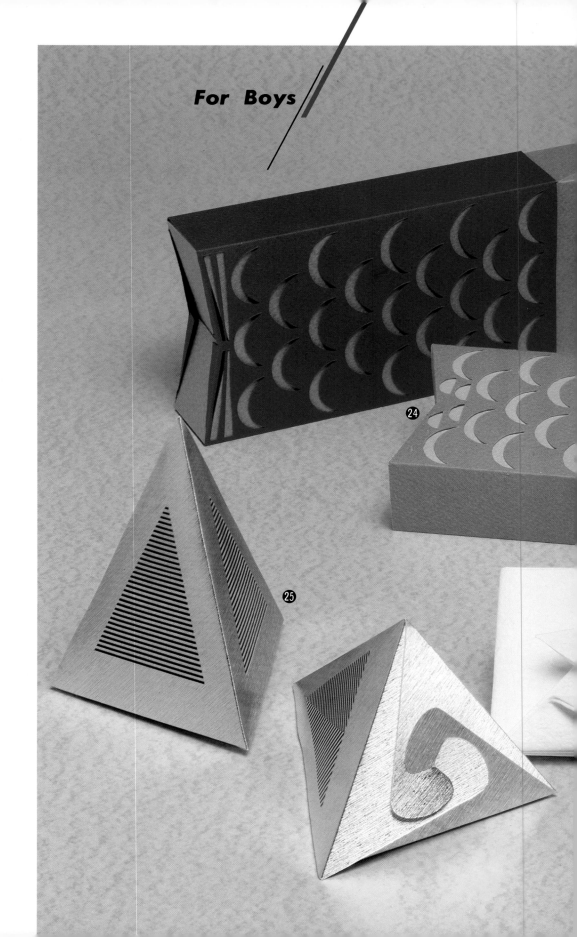

㉖

㉗

For Men

MEN'S FASHION

31

32

For Men

33

men's fashion

34

35

For Women

44

45

46

Flower Boxes

Cake Boxes

For Christmas

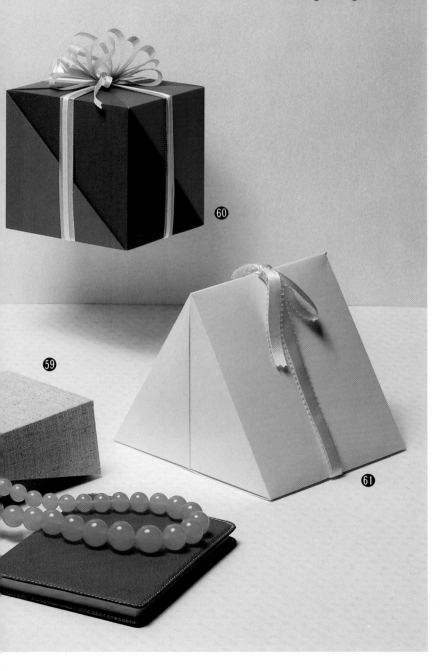

All-purpose Gift Boxes

Unique Boxes

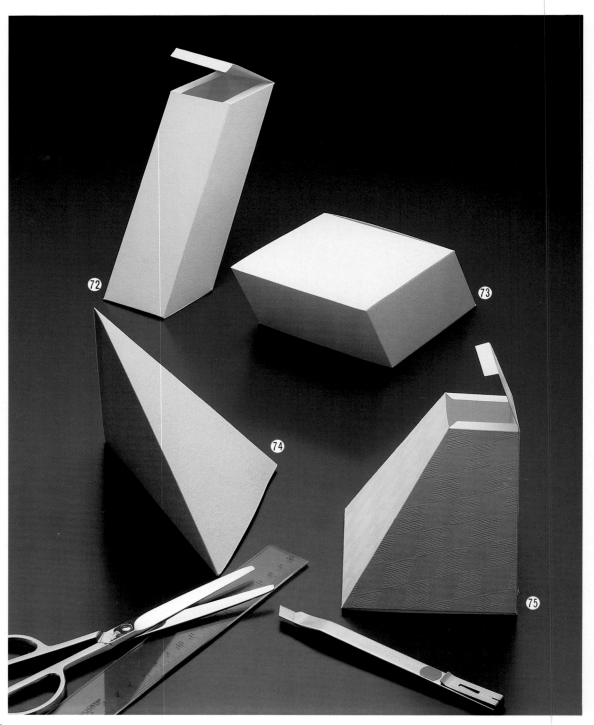

BASICS IN MAKING GIFT BOXES

Basic information about packaging

Gift Wraps:

We wrap gift packages to protect their contents, but also to show regard for the recipients, especially if a special occasion is involved. And while there are a great variety of good looking papers and boxes to choose from on the market, they offer no personal touch. They cannot enhance the thoughtfulness of a gift. And have you ever looked for an elegant way to wrap a gift of unusual size or shape!

These are all reasons to trust in and develop your own originality and creativity. Practice making some unique boxes by following the instructions in this book. Your presents will never be the same again!

Made to Measure:

The first step in making a gift box is to get the measurements down exactly: measure the size and volume of the item to be wrapped. Next, draw the unfolded shape of the container needed on drawing paper; then cut out the shape and assemble it as a sample to be sure the box will work. If it fits the gift, redraw the pattern on a paper stock of the weight needed and make the box. If there are many folds in a design, allow for the paper's thickness by drawing the pattern a bit larger. When two pieces overlap, cut the inner one a little smaller than the outer for a neat finish. These are all points to check when making the trial box.

Adjust for Weight:

The weight of the gift will determine the kind of box you make. For instance, the box for a heavy item should by made from sufficiently heavy stock and any overlapped areas should be glued securely. The tremendous variety of papers today the textures, weights, and colors will make these choices easy and fun.

Important points:

A gift box must hold the gift securely. There are some important steps to take to achieve this. First, draw the pattern of the box on the reverse side of the paper to be used (what will be the inside of the box). Then, score along the fold lines with a stencil pen, being careful not to tear the paper. Score the reverse side of the fold line (if it is folded back). After scoring, cut out the pattern and clip where nesessary. Use a craft knife and a ruler for cutting along straight lines and scissors for curved lines. To sum up these points: 1. Make the exact pattern of the box. 2. Score along the fold lines. 3. Cut and clip exactly.

Decoration:

Some gift boxes can be used as they are, but others need to be decorated. Various stickers or designed paper can be used for this purpose. You can cut out desired shapes from colored paper and glue them onto the surface or add paper craft to the box.

Various stickers:

Paper for gift boxes:

Heavy paper is mainly used for making gift boxes, but traditional Japanese rice paper can be used, too. A light-weight paper can be used for holding a small gift, but a heavy paper is needed for a heavy one. If you can not find some of the same kind of papers as shown in the book, use materials like Kent paper, thin cardboard, heavy construction paper, thin mounting card, thick cartridge paper and so on. You can also use empty boxes, in which soaps, sheets or food were packed, to make original and economical gift boxes.

Ribbon:

Ribbon is often used for gift wrapping as well as for decorating boxes. There are two kinds of ribbon; one is usually used for decorating clothes and the other for wrapping gifts. Choose a suitable ribbon for your gift, considering durability, width, color, design and so on. When deciding on a piece of ribbon, take the time to check whether it will match the gift. I do hope you will enjoy making your own gift boxes and wrappings.

STEP-BY-STEP INSTRUCTIONS
FOR FIVE BASIC GIFT BOXES

A. Quadrangular Pyramid

1. Measure the exact size of the box to be made and draw the unfolded shape.

2. Score along the fold lines with a stencil pen and a ruler.

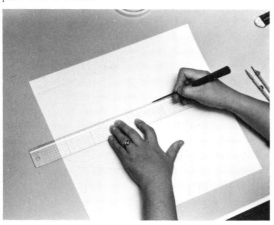

3. Cut out the shape with a craft knife and a ruler.

4. Cut-out pattern.

5. This box is tied with ribbon at the top, so punch holes.

6. Crease along scored lines.

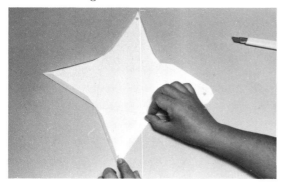

7. Crease corners carefully for a neater finish.

8. Fold forward along fold lines.

9. Fold each side piece securely with tabs folded inside.

10. Insert ribbon into two holes as shown.

11. Pass the ribbon across, joining opposite holes.

12. Tighten the ribbon and tie a knot at the top.

13. Tie into bow.

B. Square Box

1. Draw the unfolded shape of the square box and cut it out. Mark the ends of cutting lines with a stencil pen and clip up to the marks.

2. Score along fold lines with a stencil pen. Adjust pressure of the stencil pen depending on thickness of paper.

3. Fold along scored lines.

4. Crease carefully.

5. Join inner side pieces together by inserting one side into the other at slits.

6. Fold outer side pieces over inner ones.

7. Fold the lid to finish.

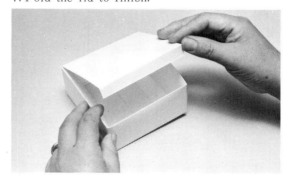

C. Variation of Triangular Box

4. Fold back the top parts of slanting sides and push each corner to fit.

1. Draw the unfolded shape of the triangular box and cut it out. Score along fold lines with a stencil pen.

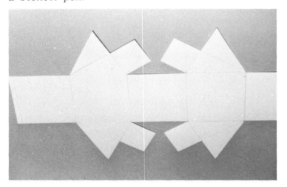

5. Now, you have a box which can be opened at the center top.

2. Fold carefully along scored lines.

6. When closed, the box becomes a triangular prism shape.

3. Crease well.

7. Finished box.

D. Cylindrical Box

1. Draw the unfolded shape and cut it out. Score along fold lines carefully with a stencil pen.

2. First, fold along vertical lines.

3. Crease fold lines.

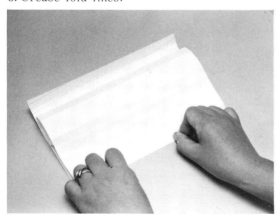

4. Next, fold along scored lines at the top and the bottom.

5. Hold folded parts with your left hand.

6. Try to make a smooth curved line.

7. Continue to fold in this way to finish.

8. All fold lines are creased.

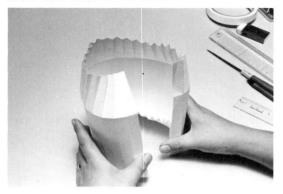

9. Apply glue (or use two-sided sticky tape) onto both ends to form tube.

10. Overlap ends.

11. Fold the top part as shown to close.

12. Fold the bottom part in the same way.

13. Finished box.

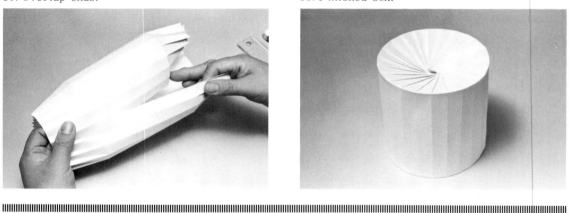

E. Wrapping for bottle

1. Decide the size of paper to be used for to the size of bottle to be wrapped. Allow about 3cm (1¼") at the top, a little longer than the radius of the bottle at the bottom, and make the width about twice the circumference of the bottle.

2. Place the bottle on the paper and secure one end of the paper with sticky tape.

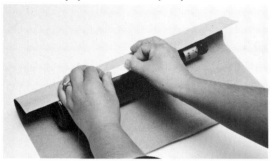

3. Cover the bottle with paper and secure the other end with two-sided sticky tape.

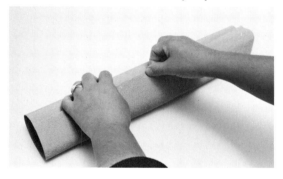

4. Fold the bottom making pleats as shown.

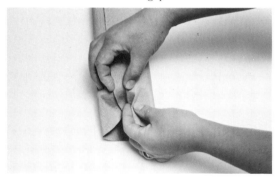

5. Push the end of the pleats into the first fold.

6. Secure the folds with a round sticker.

7. Make pleats along the neck of the bottle.

8. Check whether the pleats are even.

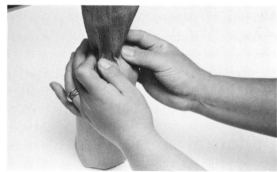

9. Tie ribbon around the neck of the bottle. Close the top of wrapping to finish.

It is advisable to add some kind of decoration for a formal gift.

INSTRUCTIONS

1 **Square Box,**
shown on page 3.

This box is made to celebrate New Year and for many other purposes.

FINISHED SIZE: Length, 13cm (5¼"). Width, 13cm (5¼"). Height, 13cm (5¼").
MATERIALS: White heavy paper, 65cm by 20cm (26"×8"); White Japanese rice paper, 65cm by 20cm (26"×8").

	Key to Lines:
Bold line ———————	Outline and cutting line.
Thin line ———————	Valley-fold line (fold forward).
Broken line – – – – –	Mountain-fold line (fold back).
Long & short Broken line —·—·—	Guide line.

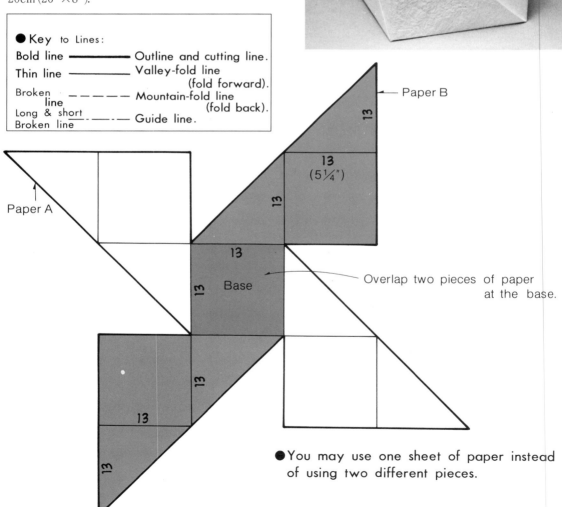

Paper B

13

13 (5¼")

13

Paper A

13

13 Base

13

13

13

13

Overlap two pieces of paper at the base.

● You may use one sheet of paper instead of using two different pieces.

② Decahedral Box,
shown on page 3.

This is suitable for packing irregular shaped gifts. You may change the color or the size of paper and use the box for a special gift.

FINISHED SIZE: One side of base and top, 16cm(6⅜")each. Height, 16cm(6⅜").
MATERIALS: Gold and purple Japanese rice paper, 80cm by 80cm(32"×32").

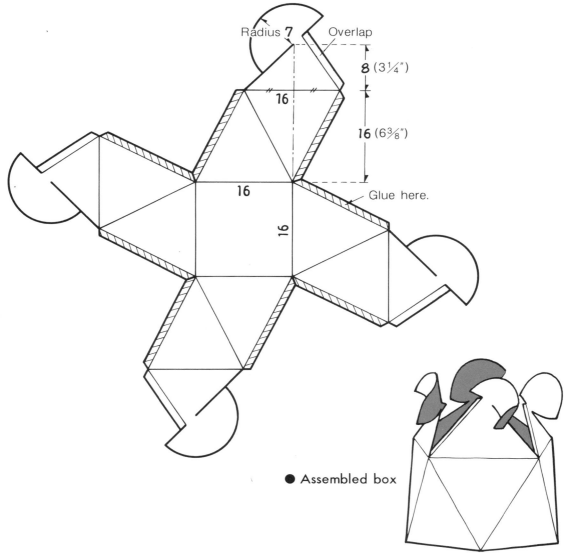

Radius 7   Overlap

8 (3¼")

16

16 (6⅜")

16

16

Glue here.

● Assembled box

③ Triangular Pyramid, shown on page 3.

This may be used as a room ornament as well as a container. Boxes of various sizes can be made.

FINISHED SIZE: One side of base, 20cm (8″). Height, 18cm (7¼″).

MATERIALS: White heavy paper, 40cm by 40cm (16″×16″). Use two sheets of paper glued together as one piece. White and red paper strings, 5 pieces of 60cm (24″) length each.

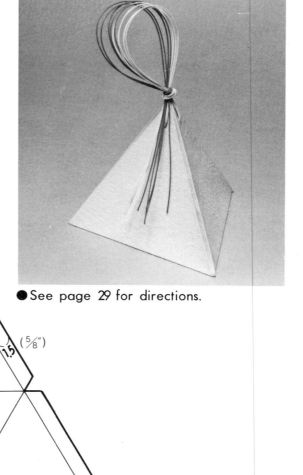

● See page 29 for directions.

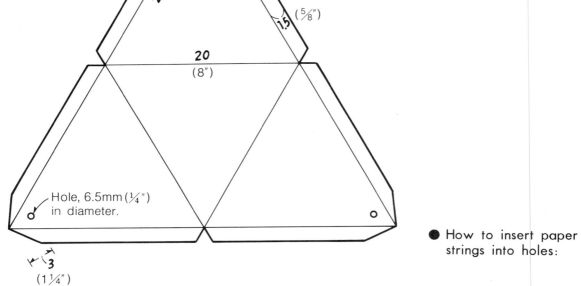

Overlap

20 20 1.5 (⅝″)

20
(8″)

Hole, 6.5mm (¼″) in diameter.

3
(1¼″)

● How to insert paper strings into holes:

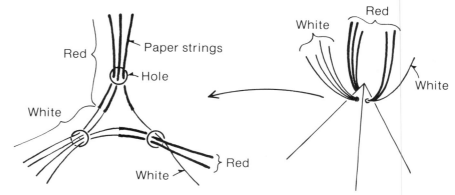

Red { Paper strings
Hole
White
White { Red
White

Red
White
White

38

4 Rectangular Box,
shown on page 3.

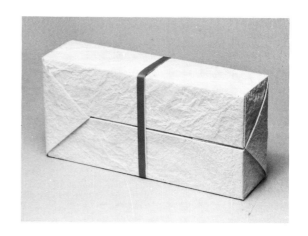

This box is opened at the center bottom, so it is suitable for packing a bottle or a gift of rectangular shape.

FINISHED SIZE: Length, 12cm (4¾"). Width, 6cm (2⅜"). Height, 24cm (9⅝").

MATERIALS: White heavy paper, 54cm by 42cm (21⅝" × 16¾"). Red and silver tapes, 1cm by 40cm (⅜" × 16") each.

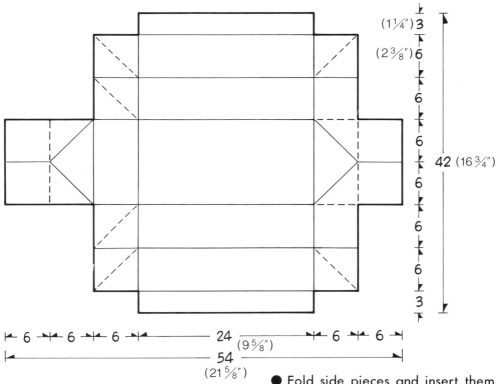

(1¼") 3
(2⅜") 6
6
6
6
6
6
3
42 (16¾")

6 6 6 24 (9⅝") 6 6
54 (21⅝")

● Crease along scored lines.

● Fold side pieces and insert them into center opening.

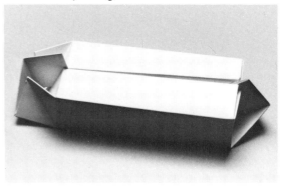

5 Wrapping for bottle, shown on page 4.

This is another method for wrapping a bottle. Following the directions on page 34, wrap the bottle with suitable paper.

FINISHED SIZE: Fits a bottle 7cm (2¾") in diameter.

MATERIALS: White heavy paper, 44cm by 37cm (17⅝"×14¾") for body. White heavy paper, 20cm by 20cm(8"×8") for top. Gold and silver paper strings, 5 pieces of 60cm(24") length each.

● Draw a circle to fit the top of the bottle.

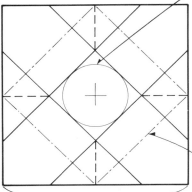

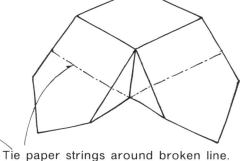

Tie paper strings around broken line.

3 to 5 times the diameter.
Adjust the size of top cover to the size of the bottle.

---

6 Square Box, shown on page 4.

Using a larger piece of paper and ribbon, this can be made in the same manner as box No. 1 shown on page 36.

FINISHED SIZE: Length, 18cm(7¼"). Width, 18cm(7¼"). Height, 18cm(7¼").

MATERIALS: White heavy paper, 90cm by 27cm (36"×10¾"); White Japanese rice paper, 90cm by 27cm(36"×10¾"). White and beige ribbons, 2cm by 100cm(¾"×40") each.

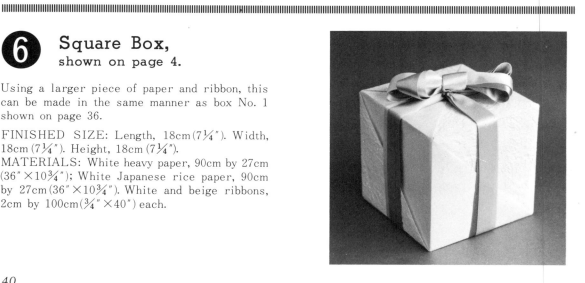

Shallow Square Box,
shown on page 4.

This box is 3cm(1¼″) deep and is suitable for packing dried food or delicacies. You may add ribbon for decoration.

FINISHED SIZE: Length, 18cm (7¼″). Width, 18cm (7¼″). Depth, 3cm (1¼″).
MATERIALS: White heavy paper, 74cm by 21cm (29⅝″×8⅜″). Red tape.

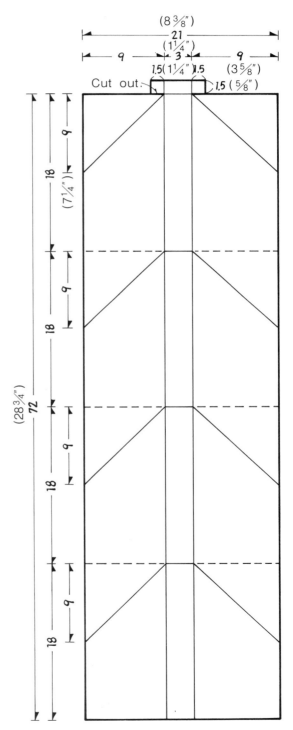

⑧ Envelope No.1,
shown on page 5.

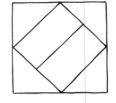

Handmade envelopes have a warm aura. They are easy to make, so try one. These envelopes hold notes folded double.

FINISHED SIZE: 9cm (3⅝″) square.
MATERIALS: White heavy Japanese rice paper, 27cm by 27cm (10¾″×10¾″). Red tape, 27cm (10¾″).

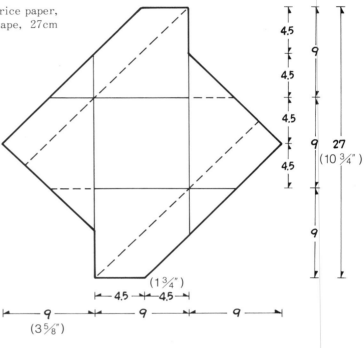

⑨ Envelope No.2,
shown on page 5.

White paper is used here, but you can change the color depending on the recipient.

FINISHED SIZE: 10cm(4") square.
MATERIALS: White heavy Japanese rice paper, 18cm by 18cm(7¼"×7¼").

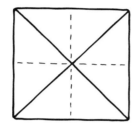

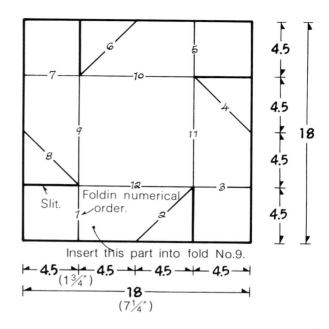

Insert this part into fold No.9.

Slit.

Foldin numerical order.

⑩ Envelope No.3,
shown on page 5.

Make maximum use of the grain of Japanese rice paper. You can make a lovely envelope with reversible paper in two colors.

FINISHED SIZE:
9cm(3⅝") square.
MATERIALS:
White heavy Japanese rice paper, 31cm by 21cm(12⅜"×8⅜").

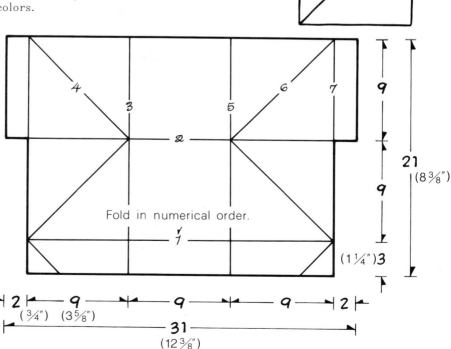

Fold in numerical order.

⑪ Envelope, No.4,

shown on page 5.

This is suitable for older people, but if you change paper you can make envelopes for all purposes.

FINISHED SIZE: 9cm by 7cm (3⅝″× 2¾″).

MATERIALS:White heavy Japanese rice paper, 26.5cm by 21 cm (10⅝″×8⅜″). White and red paper strings, 5 pieces of 30cm(12″)length each. Tie Josephine knot bringing red strings on the right side.

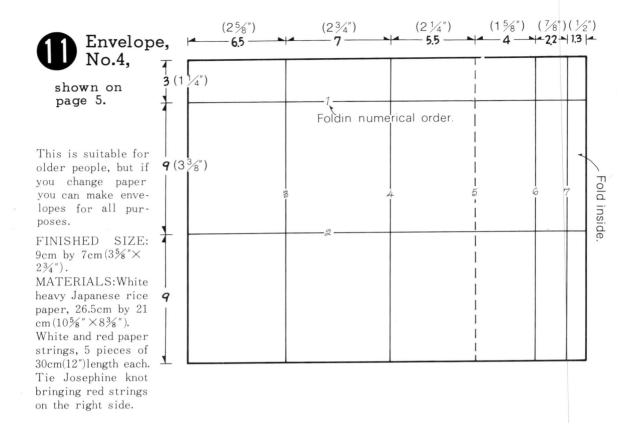

(2⅝″) (2¾″) (2¼″) (1⅝″) (⅞″) (½″)
6.5   7   5.5   4   2.2 1.3

3 (1¼″)

9 (3⅜″)

1 ——
Fold in numerical order.

3   4   5   6   7

2 ——

9

Fold inside.

Fold inside.

⑬ Chopstick Rests,
shown on page 5.

This is an elegant chopstick rest. You can use any paper you wish.

FINISHED SIZE: One side of triangle, 3cm (1¼″).

MATERIALS: Pink, yellow, light blue, charcoal gray and white heavy Japanese rice papers, 20 cm by 3cm (8″×1¼″) each. White and red Japanese rice papers for decorating chopsticks.

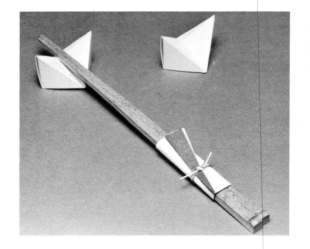

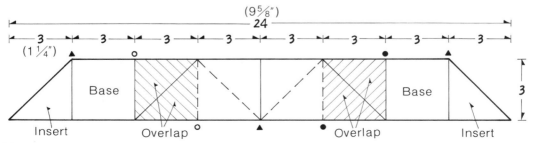

(9⅝″)
24

3   3   3   3   3   3   3   3
(1¼″)

Base   Base

Insert   Overlap   Overlap   Insert

3

12 Envelope No.5,

shown on page 5.

This is made using red and white papers. You can make envelopes for greeting cards or invitations in the same way.

FINISHED SIZE: 9cm by 7cm (3⅝″ × 2¾″).
MATERIALS: White heavy Japanese rice paper, 28cm by 23cm (11¼″ × 9¼″); red heavy Japanese rice paper, 14cm by 14cm (5⅝″ × 5⅝″). Red and white paper strings, 5 pieces of 30cm (12″) length each.

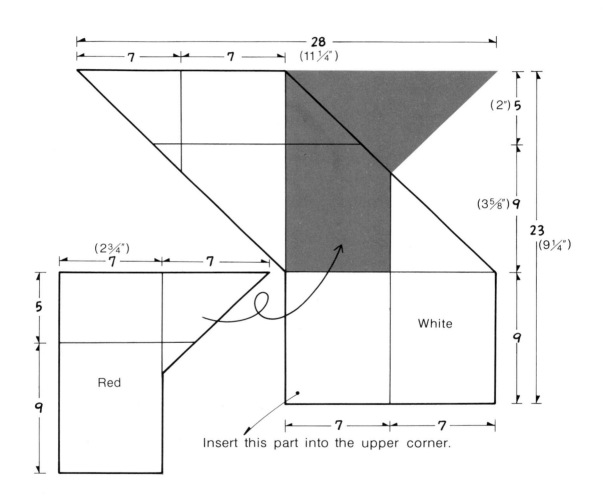

Insert this part into the upper corner.

14 Two-tone Box(deep),
shown on page 6.

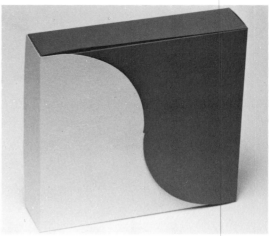

When the two hearts are closed, a dainty curved line appears on the front and back. Suitable for packing gloves, a purse or a muffler.

FINISHED SIZE: Length, 12cm(4¾"). Width, 12cm(4¾"). Depth, 2cm(¾").

MATERIALS: Red Kent paper, 28cm by 16cm (11¼"×6⅜"). White heavy Japanese rice paper, 28cm by 16cm(11¼"×6⅜"). Make two pieces using the same pattern.

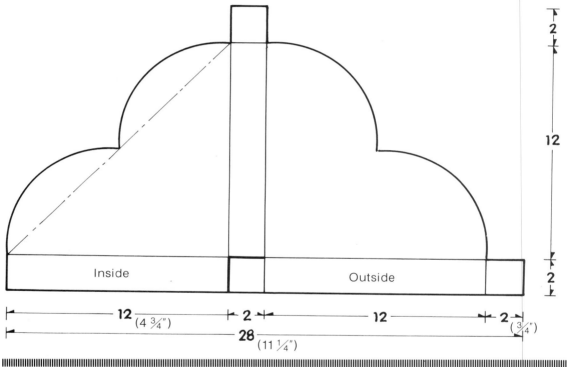

Inside   Outside

2

12

2

12 (4¾")   2   12   2 (¾")

28 (11¼")

15 Two-tone Box(shallow),
shown on page 6.

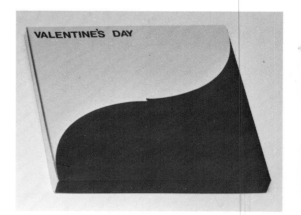

Make in the same manner as box No.14, but make the depth 1cm(⅜"). Suitable for packing handkerchiefs or a scarf.

FINISHED SIZE: Length, 12cm(4¾"). Width, 12cm(4¾"). Depth, 1cm(⅜").

MATERIALS: Chocolate and white Kent papers, 27cm by 15cm(10¾"×6") each.

16 White Box with lid,
shown on page 6.

Decorate the white box with pretty stickers and letters. Fill with assorted chocolates.

FINISHED SIZE: Length, 10cm(4″). Width, 10 cm(4″). Depth, 6cm(2⅜″).

MATERIALS: White heavy paper, 34cm by 34 cm(13⅝″×13⅝″) for box and 22cm by 18.2cm (8¾″×7¼″) for lid. Letter stickers. Heart-shaped spangles.

Box

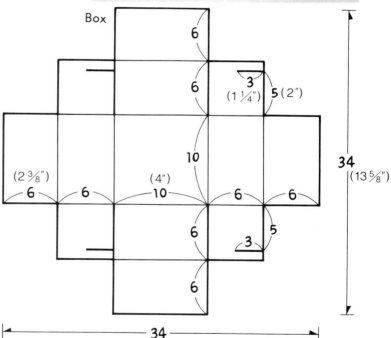

6	
6	3 (1¼″) 5 (2″)
10	
(2⅜″) 6 6 (4″) 10	6 6
6	5
3	
6	

34 (13⅝″)

34

● Various stickers

Lid

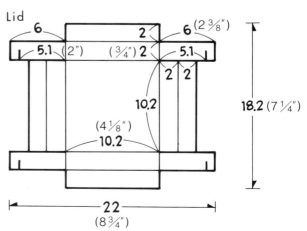

6   2   6 (2⅜″)
5.1 (2″) (¾″) 2   5.1
2 2
10.2
(4⅛″)
10.2

18.2 (7¼″)

22
(8¾″)

47

⑰ Triangular Pyramid, shown on page 7.

This dynamic box is made with wavy shapes in three colors. Suitable for packing chocolates or a belt, tiepin and cufflinks set.

FINISHED SIZE: One side of base, 7.5cm(3"). Height, 6cm (2⅜").

MATERIALS: White, dark yellow, orange and red Kent papers, 20cm by 15cm(8"×6") each. Make four pieces using the same pattern and assemble as shown below.

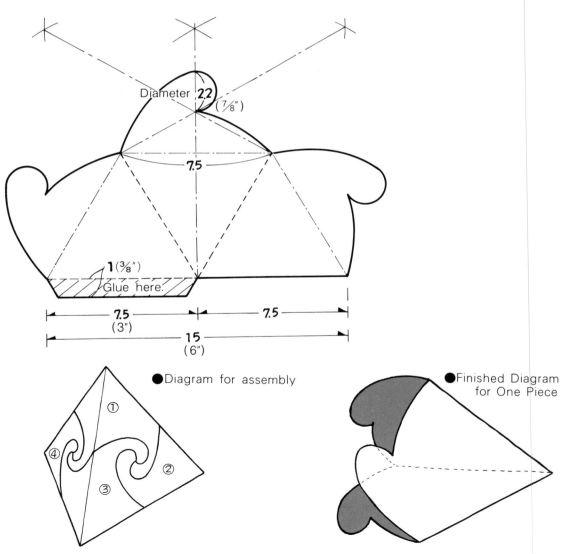

Diameter 2.2 (⅞")

7.5

1 (⅜")
Glue here.

7.5
(3")

7.5

15
(6")

●Diagram for assembly

①　②　③　④

●Finished Diagram for One Piece

18 Decahedral Box,
shown on page 7.

Make in the same manner as box No.2 shown on page 37, changing the size and paper. Use for packing something of odd shape.

FINISHED SIZE: One side of base and top, 18 cm (40″×40″). Height, 18cm (7¼″).

MATERIALS: Red embossed paper, 100cm by 100cm (40″×40″). Gold and white twisted cord, 100cm (40″).

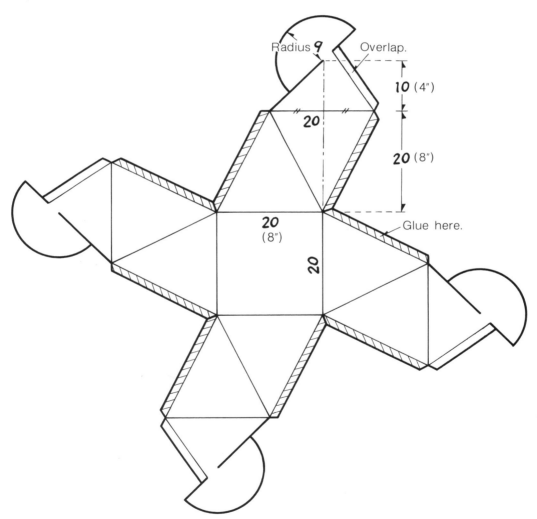

Radius **9** Overlap.

10 (4″)

20 (8″)

20

Glue here.

20
(8″)

20

Floral Box, shown on page 8.

This box resembles a peach blossom and is suitable for a candy box. Use medium-weight paper to form an elegant shape.

FINISHED SIZE: Diameter, 22cm (8¾"). Height, 7cm (2¾").

MATERIALS: White medium-weight paper, 11 cm by 11cm (4⅜"×4⅜"); Pink medium-weight paper, 11cm by 11cm (4⅜"×4⅜"). Gold ribbon, 80cm (32").

Hole for ribbon,
5mm (¼") in diameter.

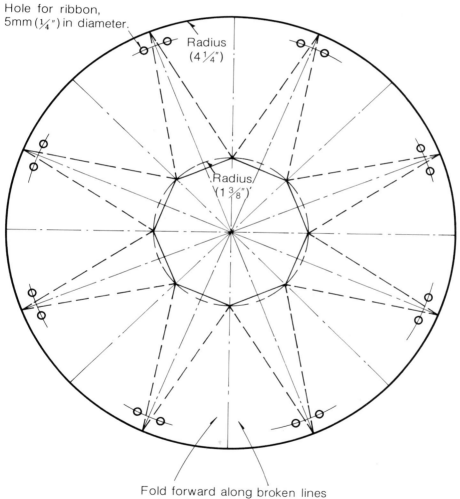

Radius (4¼")

Radius (1⅜")

Fold forward along broken lines
and make curve outward.

20 Folded Pinwheel Box,
shown on page 8.

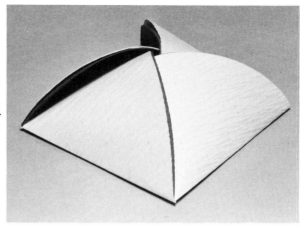

Suitable for packing sweets. Use red and white Japanese rice papers to make a dainty shape.

FINISHED SIZE: One side of base, 9cm(3⅝″).
MATERIALS: Red and white Japanese rice papers, 25cm by 25cm (10″×10″) each. Use double sheets of paper as one piece.

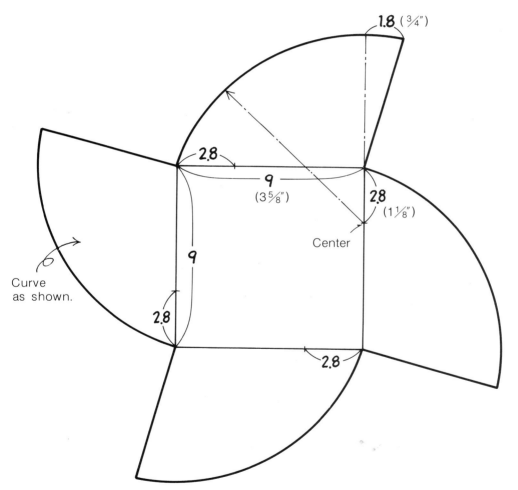

1.8 (¾″)

2.8

9
(3⅝″)

2.8
(1⅛″)

Center

9

Curve
as shown.

2.8

2.8

21 **Hexagonal Box,**
shown on page 8.

This is made of six triangular boxes. You can pack six different things.

FINISHED SIZE: One side of hexagon, 8cm (3¼"). Depth, 2.5cm (1").

MATERIALS: Peony rose heavy paper, 3 pieces of 70cm by 16cm (28"×6⅜") each. Light pink ribbon, 70cm (28").

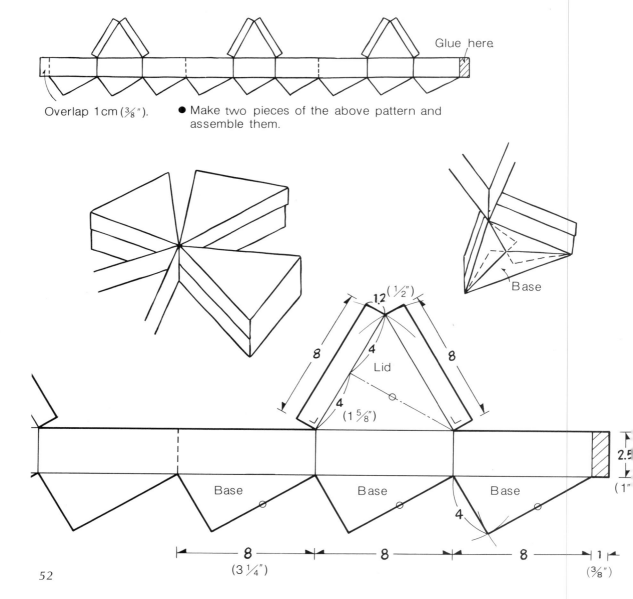

Glue here

Overlap 1cm (⅜").

● Make two pieces of the above pattern and assemble them.

1.2 (½")

8   4   8

Lid

4

(1 ⅝")

Base

Base   Base   Base

4

8   8   8   1

(3¼")

2.5

(1")

(⅜")

Quadrangular Pyramid,
shown on page 9.

Using white and pink papers, this box reminds one of Japanese "Hina" (prince and princess) dolls. Suitable for packing cookies and candies.

FINISHED SIZE: One side of base, 10cm (4"). Height, 9cm (3⅝").
MATERIALS: Rose pink and white heavy papers, 30cm by 30cm (12" × 12") each for top. Rose pink and white heavy papers, 18cm by 18cm (7¼" × 7¼") each for bottom. Red and white ribbon, 30 cm (12") length each.

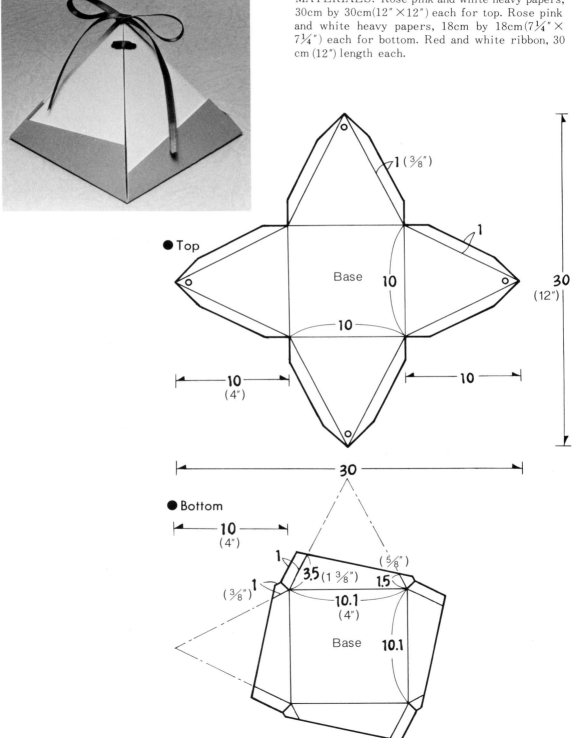

● Top

Base

1 (⅜")

1

10

10

30
(12")

10
(4")

10

● Bottom

10
(4")

30

1

3.5 (1⅜")

(⅝")

1.5

(⅜") 1

10.1
(4")

Base

10.1

23 Diamond-shaped Box,

shown on page 9.

This is made of heavy paper, so it can be stacked to save space. Make as many boxes as you can with different colors and use them at a party.

FINISHED SIZE: Longer diagonal, 12cm(4¾"). Shorter diagonal, 6cm(2⅜"). Height, 4cm(1⅝").
MATERIALS: Lavender heavy paper, 19cm by 12cm(7⅝"×4¾") for top lid. Pink heavy paper, 19cm by 12cm(7⅝"×4¾") for bottom lid. White heavy Kent paper, 27cm by 4cm(10¾"×1⅝") for side.

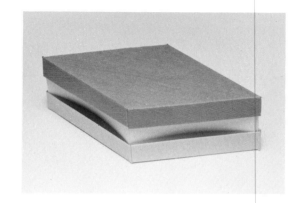

●Top or bottom lid

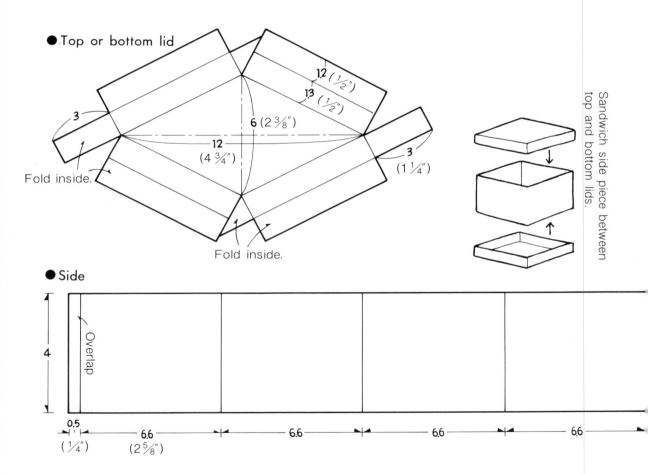

12 (½")

13 (½")

6 (2⅜")

3

12
(4¾")

Fold inside.

3
(1¼")

Fold inside.

Sandwich side piece between top and bottom lids.

●Side

Overlap

4

0.5
(¼")

6.6
(2⅝")

6.6

6.6

6.6

24 **Fish Box,** shown on page 10.

You can open the mouth of this box and put gifts in and take them out. Also a good decoration for children's rooms.

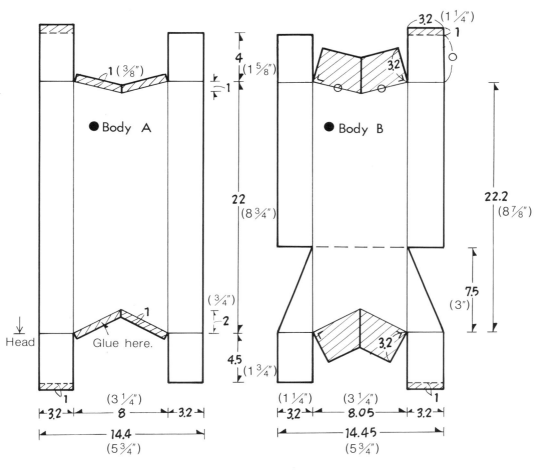

● Body A

1 ($\frac{3}{8}$")

Glue here.

Head

1

4 (1$\frac{5}{8}$")

1

22 (8$\frac{3}{4}$")

($\frac{3}{4}$")

2

4.5 (1$\frac{3}{4}$")

3.2

8 (3$\frac{1}{4}$")

3.2

14.4 (5$\frac{3}{4}$")

● Body B

3.2 (1$\frac{1}{4}$")

1

3.2

22.2 (8$\frac{7}{8}$")

7.5 (3")

3.2

(1$\frac{1}{4}$") 3.2

(3$\frac{1}{4}$") 8.05

1

(1$\frac{1}{4}$") 3.2

14.45 (5$\frac{3}{4}$")

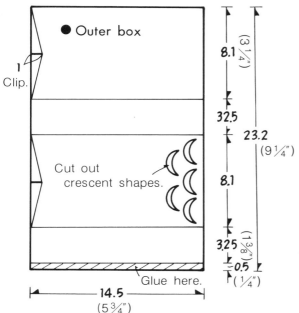

● Outer box

1 Clip.

Cut out crescent shapes.

Glue here.

8.1 (3$\frac{1}{4}$")

32.5

23.2 (9$\frac{1}{4}$")

8.1

3.25 (1$\frac{3}{8}$")

0.5 ($\frac{1}{4}$")

14.5 (5$\frac{3}{4}$")

FINISHED SIZE: Length, 22.2cm (8$\frac{7}{8}$"). Height, 8.1cm (3$\frac{1}{4}$"). Depth, 3.2cm(1$\frac{1}{4}$").
MATERIALS: Green or bright yellow Kent paper, 14.5cm by 32.5cm(5$\frac{3}{4}$"×13") for body A. Navy or orange Kent paper, 14.5cm by 32cm(5$\frac{3}{4}$" ×12$\frac{3}{4}$") for body B. Navy or orange Kent paper, 14.5cm by 22.6cm(5$\frac{3}{4}$"×9")for outer box. Scraps of navy and orange Kent paper for eyes.

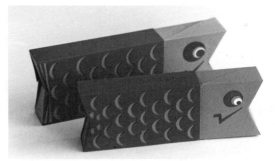

㉕ Triangular Pyramid, shown on page 10.

This is modeled after a traditional package for Japanese food. Suitable for packing candies or miniature cars.

FINISHED SIZE: Height, 8.5cm (3⅜"). One side of base, 8cm (3¼").

MATERIALS: Gold and silver heavy papers, 22cm by 15cm (8¾"×6") each. Striped paper for decoration.

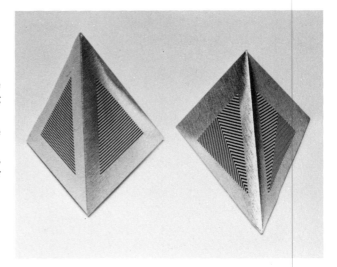

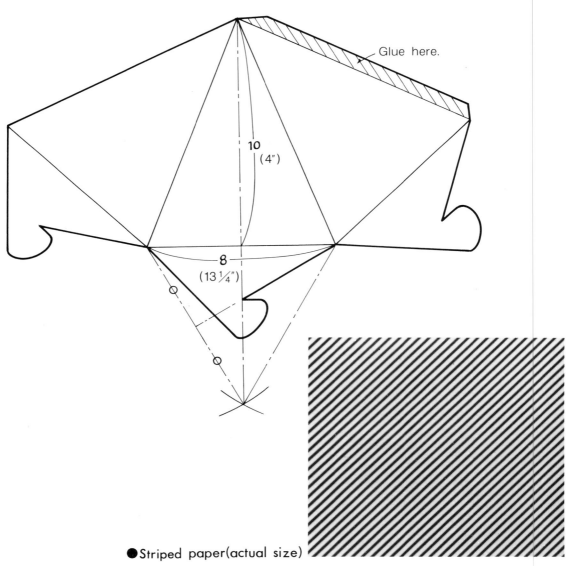

Glue here.

10
(4")

8
(13¼")

●Striped paper(actual size)

㉖ Carton Box,
shown on page 11.

The height of this box is adjustable, so you can make long or short boxes. Change the design of the lid and make a unique box.

FINISHED SIZE: Long box: Length, 6cm(2⅜″). Width, 6cm(2⅜″). Height, 10cm(4″). Short box: Length, 6cm(2⅜″). Width, 6cm(2⅜″). Height, 7 cm(2¾″).

MATERIALS: Blue and green checked heavy paper, 14cm by 14cm(5⅝″×5⅝″) for top and bottom lids. Heavy cardboard, 25cm by 10cm (10″×4″) or 7cm(2¾″) for side. Blue and green checked paper for decoration. Gold and silver twisted cords, 80cm(32″) each.

● The pattern below is for the long box.

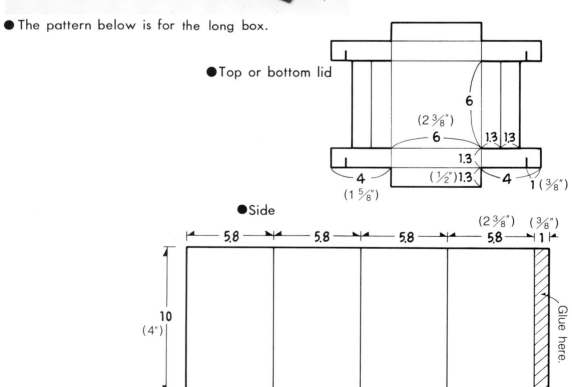

●Top or bottom lid

●Side

27 **Helmet,** shown on page 11.

You may use this bag not only as a container but also for a decoration. It looks good if you make it with heavy Japanese rice paper.

FINISHED SIZE: Length, 6.5cm (2⅝"). Width, 12.5cm (5").
MATERIALS: White heavy Japanese rice paper, 36.4 cm by 25.5cm (14½" × 10¼").

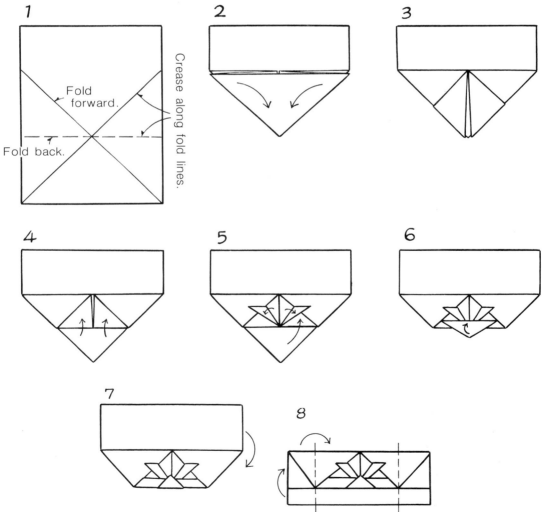

28 Trapezoid Box, shown on page 12.

This box can hold various gifts, but is most suitable for packing gifts for men. How about using this for sending electric goods or men's jewelry?

FINISHED SIZE: Base, 10cm by 18cm (4"×7¼"). Top, 8cm by 16cm(3¼"×6⅜"). Height, 6cm(2⅜").
MATERIALS: : Light blue metallic paper, 48cm by 40cm(19¼"×16"). Striped paper and ribbon for decoration.

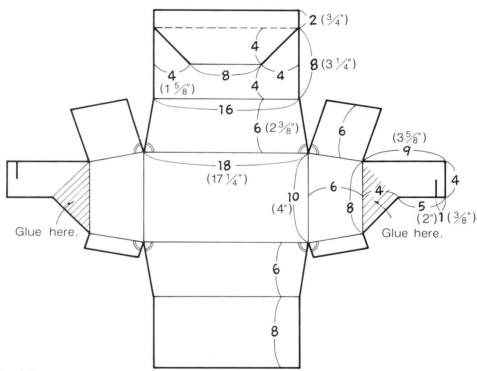

● How to attach ribbon.

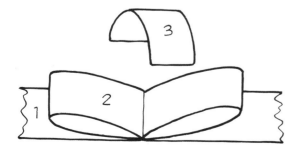

29 Bottle Box, shown on page 12.

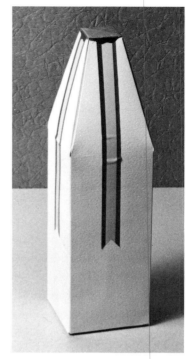

This box is suitable for a wine or a beer bottle. Change the height and size of base according to the size of bottle to be packed.

FINISHED SIZE: Base, 8cm(3¼") square. Height, 30cm(12").

MATERIALS: White heavy paper, 40cm by 33 cm(16"×13¼"). Colored paper or stickers for decoration.

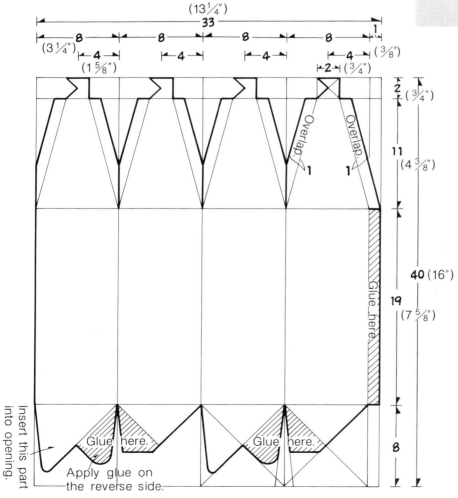

Overlap. Overlap.

Glue here.

Glue here. Glue here.

Apply glue on the reverse side.

Insert this part into opening.

(13¼")
33
8 8 8 8 1
(3¼")
4 4 4 4 (³⁄₈")
2 (¾")

2 (¾")
11 (4³⁄₈")
1 1
40 (16")
19 (7⁵⁄₈")
8

30 Flat Box, shown on page 12.

Suitable for packing a silk muffler or handkerchiefs. You can make a bigger box by changing
depth.

FINISHED SIZE: Length, 20cm(8″). Width, 20
cm(8″). Depth, 0.5cm(¼″).
MATERIALS: Dark brown heavy paper, 46.5cm
by 38cm(18⅝″×15¼″).

Cut out a design from wrapping paper and glue
onto the surface for decoration.

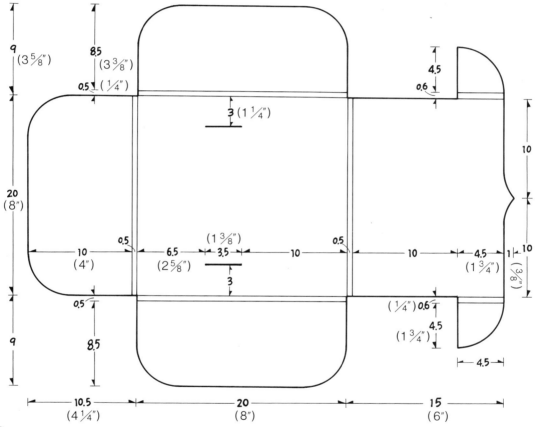

33 Flat Box, shown on page 14.

Make in the same manner as box No. 30, changing
the trimmings. The finished box looks quite
different from the above.

FINISHED SIZE: Length, 20cm(8″). Width, 20
cm(8″). Depth, 0.5cm(¼″).
MATERIALS: Cream heavy paper, 46.5cm by
38cm(18⅝″×15¼″). Dark and light blue ribbons,
60cm(24″). Checked paper for decoration. Sticker.

31 Box for Necktie,
shown on page 13.

This box will enhance the beauty of a necktie. Try to make attractive designs with stickers and colorful paper.

FINISHED SIZE: Length, 30cm (12″). Width, 15 cm (6″). Height, 4cm (1⅝″).

MATERIALS: Green heavy paper, 38cm by 31 cm (15¼″ × 12⅜″). Dark green heavy paper, 60cm by 7cm (24″ × 2¾″). Stickers.

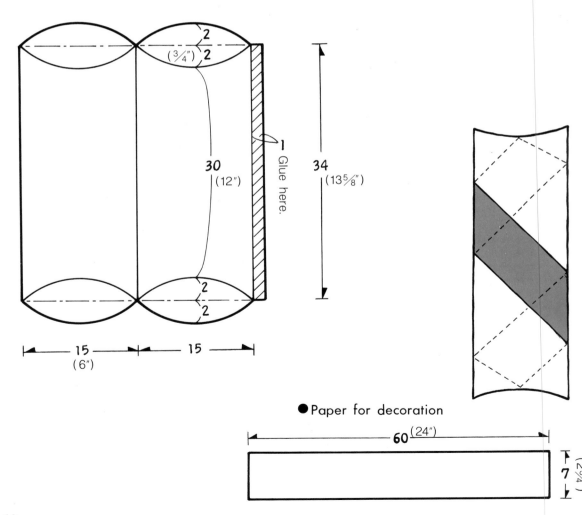

2
2
(¾″)

30
(12″)

Glue here.
1

34
(13⅝″)

15
(6″)

15

2
2

● Paper for decoration

60 (24″)

7
(2¾″)

32 Book-style Box,
shown on page 13.

This is modeled after a book slipcase and can be used for many purposes. Change the color of paper according to the recipient.

FINISHED SIZE: Length, 18cm(7¼"). Width, 15cm(6"). Depth, 3cm(1¼").
MATERIALS: Silver heavy paper, 33cm by 32cm(13¼"×12¾") for inner box. Turquoise heavy paper, 50cm by 18cm (20"× 7¼") for outer box. Cut chosen design out your desired of outer box.

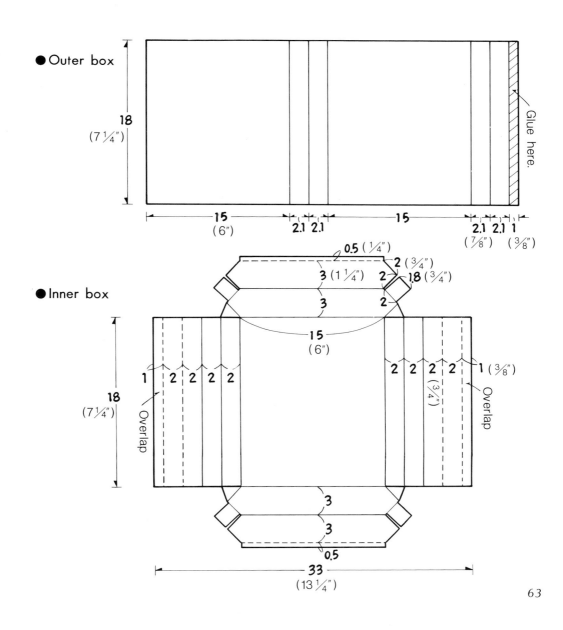

● Outer box

18 (7¼")

Glue here.

15 (6") 2.1 2.1 15 2.1 2.1 1
(⅞") (⅜")

● Inner box

0.5 (¼")
2 (¾")
3 (1¼") 2 1.8 (¾")
3 2
15 (6")
1 2 2 2 2   2 2 2 2 1 (⅜")
18 (7¼")
Overlap (¾") Overlap
3
3
0.5
33 (13¼")

34 Sock Case,
shown on page 14.

Socks are often given as a gift, so this box will enhance the present for a special person. Try to change trimmings and colors of paper.

FINISHED SIZE: Length, 27cm(10 ¾″). Width, 12cm(4¾″). Depth, 2cm (¾″).

MATERIALS: Pink textured heavy paper, 41cm by 22.5cm(16⅜″×9″) for inner case. Blue textured heavy paper, 31cm by 28cm(12⅜″×11¼″) for outer case. Stickers.

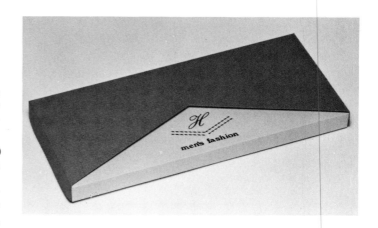

●Outer case　　　　　　　　　　　●Inner case

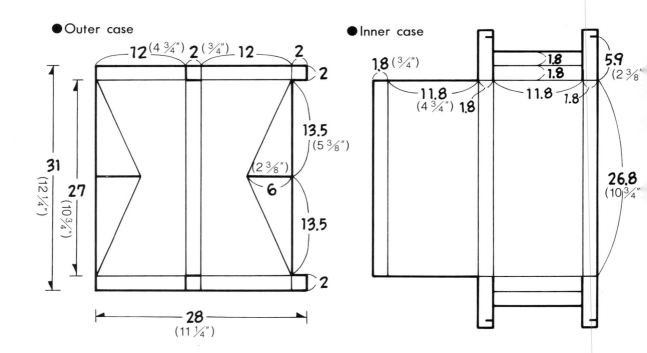

35 Triangle Box,

shown on page 14.

Suitable for packing small accessories or a watch. Decorate the lid with bright trimmings for younger people.

FINISHED SIZE: One side of triangle, 12cm (4¾″). Depth, 3.5cm(1⅜″).
MATERIALS: Lavender textured heavy paper, 37cm by 28cm(14¾″×11¼″). Stickers.

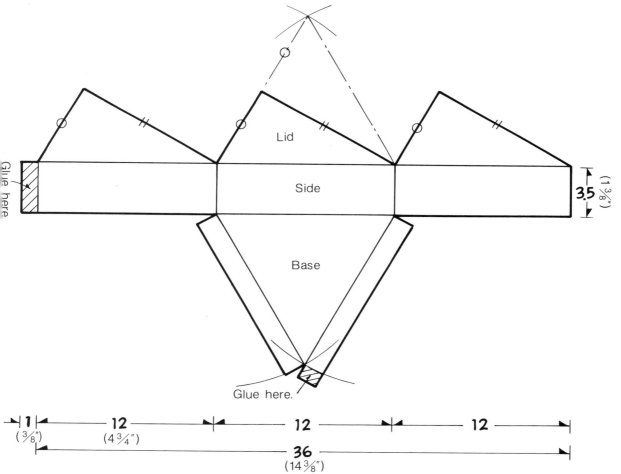

36 Bag-style Box,
shown on page 15.

You may use this box as a handbag. The box has considerable capacity, so it can be used for many purposes.

FINISHED SIZE: Length, 18.5cm (7⅜"). Width, 30cm (12"). Depth, 5cm (2").

MATERIALS: Navy heavy paper, 58cm by 36cm (23¼"×14⅜") for inner box. Dark red heavy paper, 56cm by 40cm (22⅜"× 16") for outer box. White ribbon. Stickers.

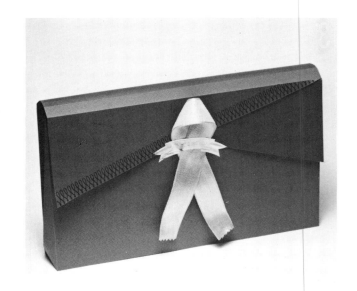

● Outer box

Base

10 (4")
5
18 (7¼")
2.5
2.5
2.5
2.5 (1")
5
18

|←5→| (2")   30 (12") |←5→|

● Inner box

10 (4")
4.9 (2")
17.8 (7⅛")
(1") 2.5
4.9
1 (⅜")
Glue here.
17.8
(1¼") 3   4.9

29.8 (12")

Fold back.

37 Flat Box No.1,
shown on page 15.

Suitable for packing something unusual. This cannot hold a bulky gift, but it has a very impressive air.

FINISHED SIZE: Length, 10cm(4"). Width, 10cm(4"). Depth, same thickness as the paper.
MATERIALS: Pink heavy Japanese rice paper, 60cm by 40cm(24"×16"). Metallic ribbon, 45cm(18").

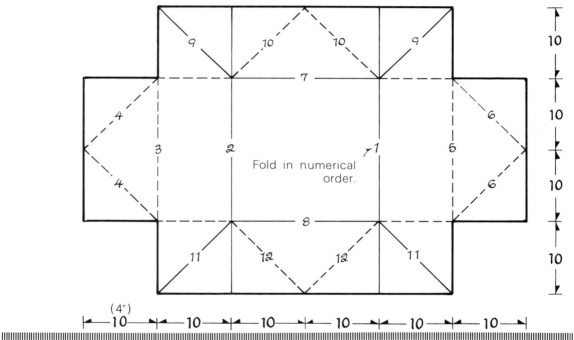

Fold in numerical order.

10

10

10

10

(4")
10 — 10 — 10 — 10 — 10 — 10

38 Flat Box No.2,
shown on page 15.

Make in same manner as the above, but halve the length and width.

FINISHED SIZE: Length, 5cm(2"). Width, 5cm (2"). Depth, same thickness as the paper.
MATERIALS: Cream and purple heavy Japanese rice papers, 30cm by 20cm(12"×8") each. Red and pink ribbons, 20cm(8") each.

39 Paper Bag,
shown on page 16.

There are many ready-made paper bags on the market, however, if you make them yourself, you can change the size and color of paper freely. Try to make various bags.

FINISHED SIZE: Length, 30.5cm(12¼"). Width, 20cm(8"). Depth, 4cm(1⅝").

MATERIALS: Navy textured paper, 30.5cm by 49.5cm(12¼"×19¾"). Gold, silver and red papers for weaving, 1.5cm by 50cm(⅝"×20") each. Stickers.

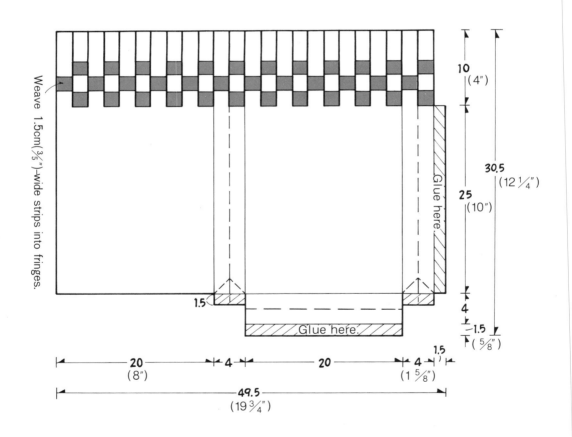

40 Hexagonal Box,
shown on page 16.

This can be reused as a bag. Use colored paper when sending to younger people.

FINISHED SIZE: Diameter, 24cm (9⅝"). Depth, 3cm (1¼").

MATERIALS: Cream heavy paper, 76cm by 35 cm (30⅜"×14"). Red tape for handle, 100cm (40").

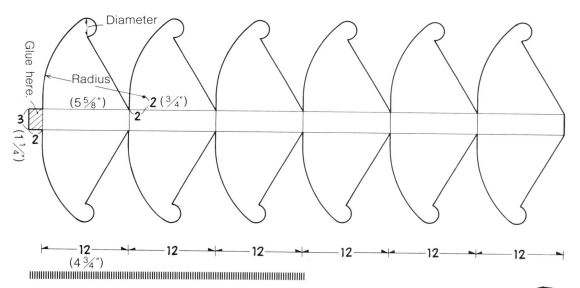

Diameter

Glue here.

Radius

(5⅝")

2 (¾")

2

3

(1¼")

2

12 (4¾") ── 12 ── 12 ── 12 ── 12 ── 12

41 Hexagonal Box,
shown on page 17.

Make as the above box, changing the color of ribbon to navy.

● Detail for center

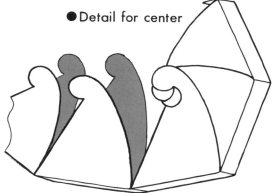

42 Cylindrical Box,
shown on page 17.

This box may be used for packing various things but not heavy articles. You can make a hat box in the same manner, changing the size.

FINISHED SIZE: Diameter, 12cm (4¾"). Height, 15cm (6").
MATERIALS: White heavy paper, 26cm by 40cm (10⅜" ×16"). Pink ribbon, 80cm (32").
See page 33 for directions.

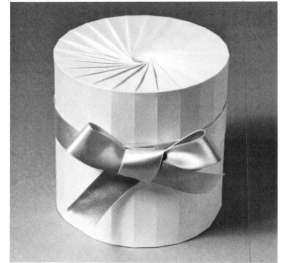

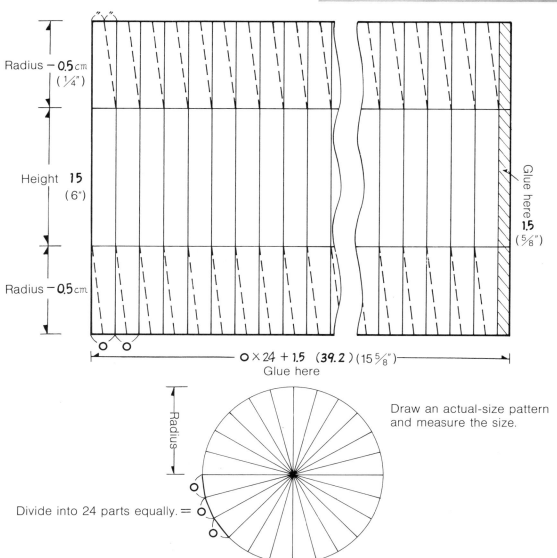

Radius — 0.5 cm (¼")

Height 15 (6")

Radius — 0.5 cm

Glue here 1.5 (⅝")

○ × 24 + 1.5 (39.2) (15⅝")
Glue here

Radius

Divide into 24 parts equally. =

Draw an actual-size pattern and measure the size.

43 Square Box with floral design, shown on page 17.

When you cannot find heavy-weight patterned paper like this, try using double sheets of paper, one solid and the other patterned or colored.

FINISHED SIZE: Length, 10cm (4"). Width, 10 cm (4"). Height, 10cm (4").

MATERIALS: Heavy patterned paper, 49cm by 43cm (19⅝"×17¼"). Dark purple tape, 45cm (18").

Make a 10cm (4") cube with white heavy construction paper. Put the gift in and clse with sticky tape. Then, cut out the pattern from thin wrapping paper or Japanese rice paper to add a little fullness and cover the box with this.

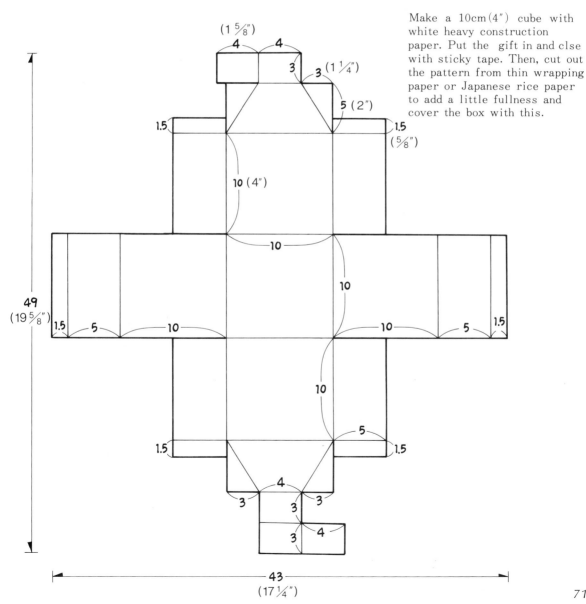

Pentagonal Flower Box,
shown on page 18.

Adjust the length of the box to fit the flowers.

FINISHED SIZE: One side of pentagon, 7cm (2¾"). Length, 33cm (13 ¼").

MATERIALS: Yellow-green heavy paper, 15cm by 60cm (6"×24") for inner box. White heavy paper, 33 cm by 38cm (13¼"×15¼") for outer box. Yellow-green heavy paper, 18 cm by 38cm (7¼"×15¼") for decoration. Various white dots cut from white paper. Gold ribbon, 80cm (32").

● Inner box

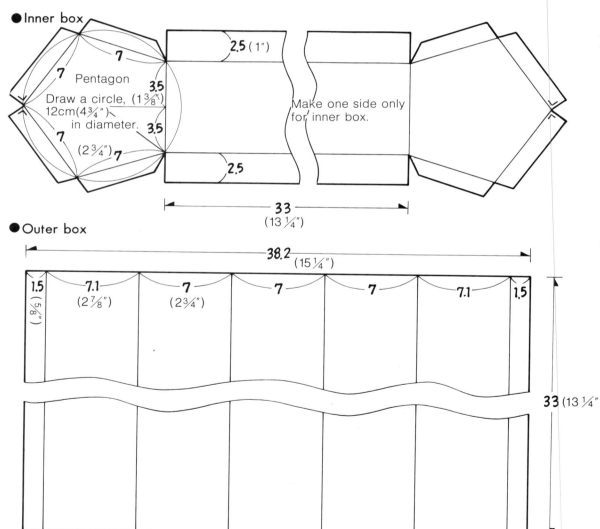

●Outer box

72

45 Wrapping for Transparent Acrylic Box,

shown on page 18.

A transparent acrylic box is good for packing a corsage. Make the most of the box to show off the pretty things inside. Decorate the box with a bright ribbon.

FINISHED SIZE: Fits 12cm (4¾") square box.
MATERIALS: Light green heavy paper, 60cm by 24cm (24"×9⅝"). Silver ribbon, two different widths.

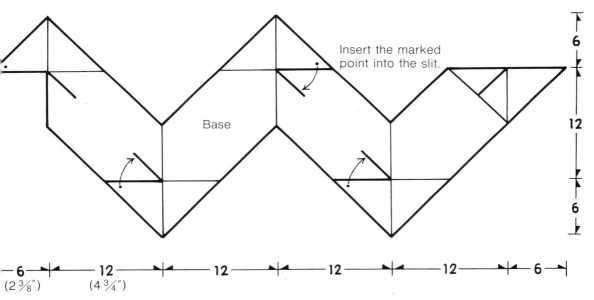

Insert the marked point into the slit.

Base

6

12

6

—6—→|←——12——→|←——12——→|←——12——→|←——12——→|←—6—→|
(2⅜")   (4¾")

●Tips for wrapping a transparent box:

There are several kinds of transparent boxes made of plastics (acrylics or celluloid) or glass. Make the most of these clear boxes by wrapping partially to show off the inside. It is great fun to see beautiful things through a box like the above for the sender as well as the recipient. The shapes of transparent boxes are varied — cubes, rectangles, triangular pyramids, cylinders, globes and so on. Some have light colors such as blue, green, pink or yellow. Choose the most suitable box and ribbon for the gift, considering its shape, color and materials of the box. Close the lid with clear sticky tape.

⁴⁶ Flower Box with Handles, shown on page 18.

This is a hexagonal box with handles. Choose the color of the paper to match the flowers.

FINISHED SIZE: One side of hexagon, 5cm (2″). Length, 25cm (10″).

MATERIALS: Rose pink heavy paper, 40cm by 33cm (16″×13¼″) for inner box. White heavy paper, 42cm by 25cm (16¾″×10″) for outer box. Stickers.

● Outer box

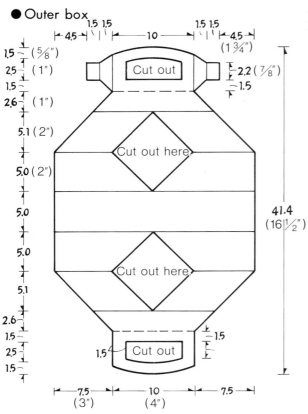

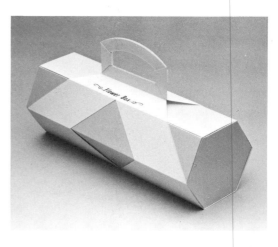

● Inner box

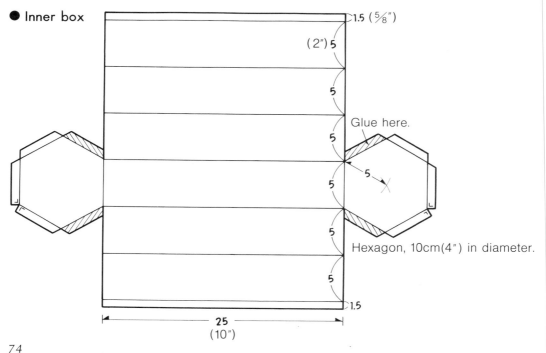

Glue here.

Hexagon, 10cm(4″) in diameter.

74

47 Cake Box No.1,

shown on page 19.

This box can hold plenty of cakes.

FINISHED SIZE: Length, 20.2cm (8⅛″). Width, 20.2cm (8⅛″). Height, 10.1cm (4″).

MATERIALS: White Kent paper, 63cm by 44cm (25¼″×17⅝″) for inner box. White heavy paper, 77.4cm by 40.4cm (31″×16⅛″) for outer box. Stickers.

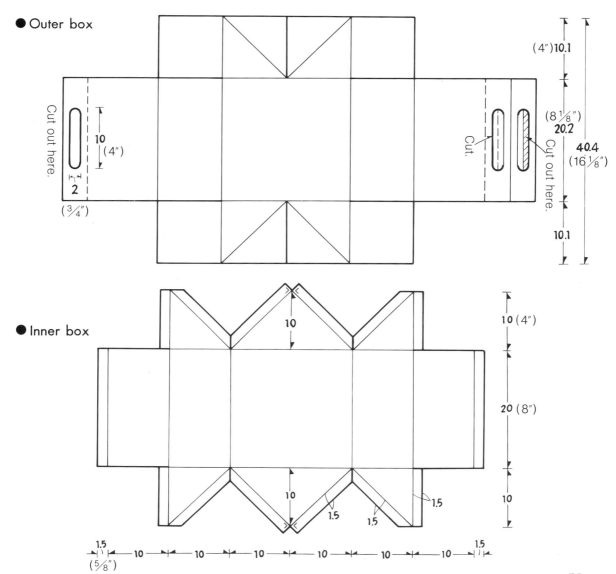

● Outer box

Cut out here.

10 (4″)

2 (¾″)

Cut.

Cut out here.

(4″)10.1

(8⅛″) 20.2

40.4 (16⅛″)

10.1

● Inner box

10 (4″)

20 (8″)

10

10

10

1.5

1.5

1.5

1.5

1.5 (5/8″) 10 10 10 10 10 10 1.5

48 Cake Box No.2,
shown on page 19.

Use this elegant box for sending a loaf cake.

FINISHED SIZE: Base, 8cm by 18cm (3¼″×7¼″). Height excluding handle, about 9cm (3⅝″).
MATERIALS: Light cream heavy paper, 52cm by 33cm (20¾″×13¼″). Stickers.

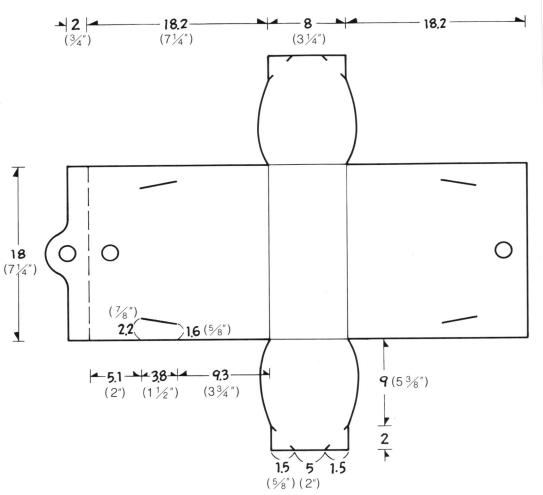

2 (¾″)   18.2 (7¼″)   8 (3¼″)   18.2

18 (7¼″)

(⅞″)
2.2   1.6 (⅝″)

5.1 (2″)   3.8 (1½″)   9.3 (3¾″)

9 (5⅜″)

2

1.5   5   1.5
(⅝″) (2″)

49 Cake Box No.3,
shown on page 19.

Good for holding small cakes or as souvenir boxes for a party. Tie with a pretty ribbon.

FINISHED SIZE: Base, 15cm(6″)square. Height, 13cm (5¼″).

MATERIALS: Rose pink heavy paper, 79cm by 24cm (31⅝″×9⅝″). Blue ribbon, 70cm (28″). See page 32 for directions.

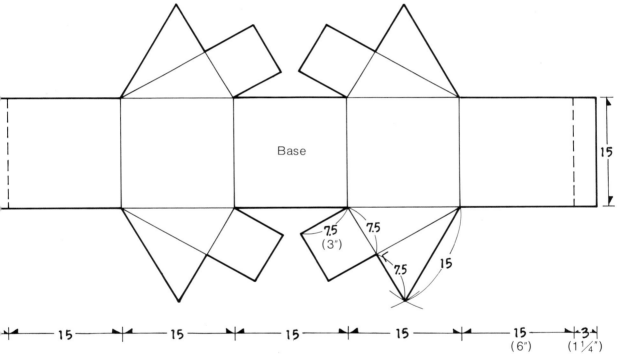

Base

15

7.5 (3″) 7.5

7.5

15

15   15   15   15   15 (6″) 3 (1¼″)

61 Triangular Box,
shown on page 23.

This box is opened at the center top, so it is easy to take out the things inside. Make the box with white paper and tie with pink ribbon. Use the same pattern as the above box.

FINISHED SIZE: Base, 15cm(6″)square. Height, 13cm (5¼″).

MATERIALS: White Kent paper, 79cm by 24cm (31⅝″×9⅝″). Pink ribbon, 70cm (28″).

50 House-shaped Box with Starry Roof,

shown on page 20.

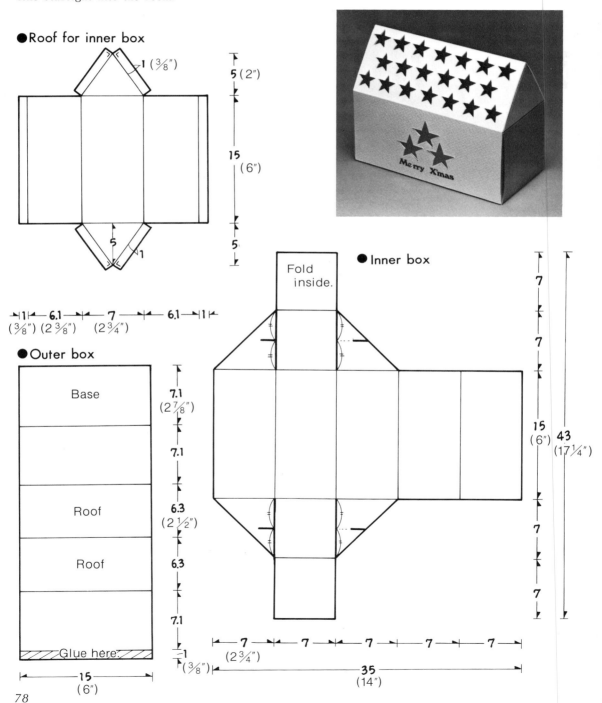

shown on page 20.

FINISHED SIZE: Length, 15cm (6"). Width, 7.1 cm (2⅞"). Height, 12cm (4¾").

MATERIALS: Silver heavy paper, 43cm by 35 cm (17¼"×14") for inner box. Silver heavy paper, 29cm by 22cm (11⅝"×8¾") for roof. White heavy paper, 15cm by 34cm (6"×13⅝") for outer box. Stickers.

Beautiful packages piled under the Christmas tree make Christmas Eve more delightful. Silver paper used for the inside of the box will reflect like starlight into the room.

● **Roof for inner box**

1 (⅜")

5 (2")

15 (6")

5

1

⟵1⟶⟵6.1⟶⟵ 7 ⟶⟵ 6.1 ⟶⟵1⟶
(⅜") (2⅜") (2¾")

● **Outer box**

Base	7.1 (2⅞")
	7.1
Roof	6.3 (2½")
Roof	6.3
	7.1
Glue here.	1 (⅜")

⟵ 15 (6") ⟶

● **Inner box**

Fold inside.

7

7

15 (6") 43 (17¼")

7

7

⟵ 7 ⟶⟵ 7 ⟶⟵ 7 ⟶⟵ 7 ⟶⟵ 7 ⟶
(2¾")

⟵ 35 (14") ⟶

78

● Cut out star shapes from the roof following the diagrams at right.

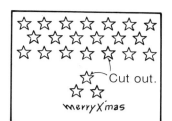

Cut out.
merry X'mas

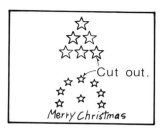

Cut out.
Merry Christmas

51 Hexagonal Pyramid with Santa Claus,
shown on page 20.

It is easy to make this box, but you may need more time to make Santa Claus. Try to make a charming one.

FINISHED SIZE: Diameter of base, about 9.6 cm (3⅞"). Height, 14.5cm (5¾").

MATERIALS: Red heavy paper, 22cm by 32cm (8¾"×12¾"). White Kent paper, 10cm by 10cm (4"×4").

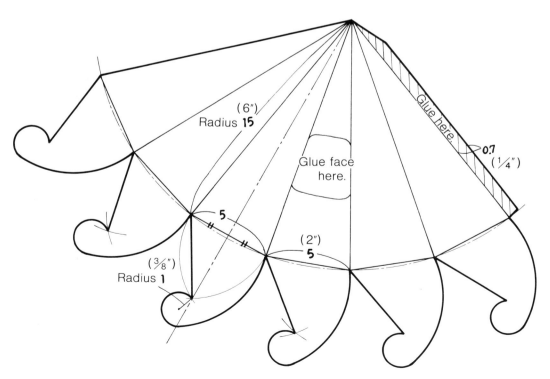

(6")
Radius **15**

Glue here.

Glue face here.

0.7
(¼")

5

(2")
5

(⅜")
Radius **1**

52 Thin Square Box,
shown on page 20.

Gold and silver papers are used for this Christmas gift box, but by changing the color, you can use it for any formal occasion.

FINISHED SIZE: Length, 15cm (6″). Width, 15 cm(6″). Depth, 2cm(¾″).
MATERIALS: Silver heavy paper, 50cm by 32 cm(20″×12¾″). Gold heavy paper, 50cm by 15cm (20″×6″). Vermilion ribbon, 100cm (40″).

●Pattern for gold paper

●Pattern for silver paper

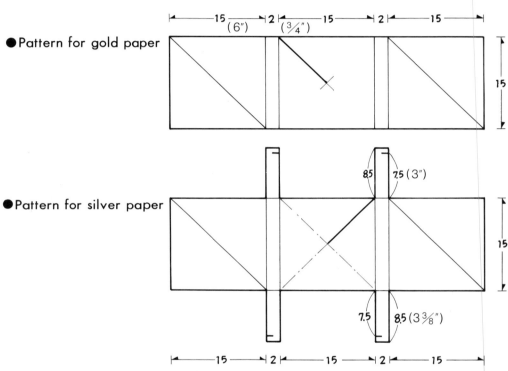

53 Christmas Bag,
shown on page 20.

Make an ordinary paper bag and decorate it with star-shaped spangles and colorful stickers.

FINISHED SIZE: Length, 22cm (8¾″). Width, 18cm (7¼″). Depth, 5cm (2″).
MATERIALS: Red textured paper, 47.5cm by 28.5cm (19″×11⅜″). Star-shaped spangles. Colorful stickers.

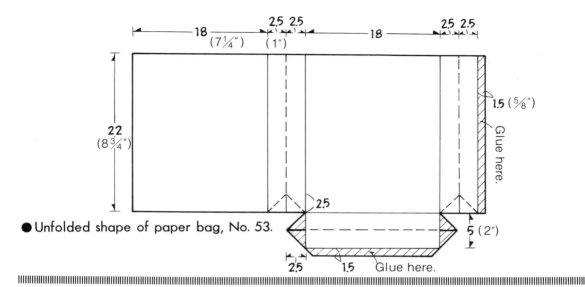

● Unfolded shape of paper bag, No. 53.

 54 **Toy Box,** shown on page 21.

This is the type of box that is often used at pastry stores. Decorate the box with various stickers.

FINISHED SIZE: Length, 20cm (8"). Width, 20 cm (8"). Height, 13cm (5¼").
MATERIALS: White heavy paper, 70cm by 48 cm (28"×19¼"). Stickers.

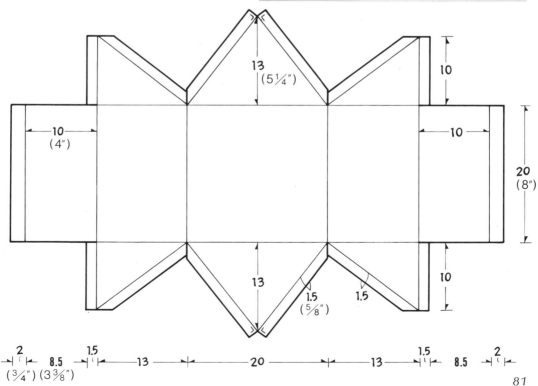

**House-shaped Box
with Starry Roof,**
shown on page 21.

FINISHED SIZE: Same as box No. 50.
MATERIALS: Gold heavy paper, 43cm by 35cm
($17\frac{1}{4}$"×14") for inner box. Gold heavy paper, 29
cm by 22cm ($11\frac{5}{8}$"×$8\frac{3}{4}$") for roof. Red heavy
paper, 15cm by 34cm (6"×$13\frac{5}{8}$") for outer box.
Stickers.

Use the same pattern as box No. 50. Change the
color of paper and design of the outer box.

 Variation of Trapezoid Box,
shown on page 22.

This is a unique design for a gift box, for it not
only holds the gift perfectly but also draws
everybody's attention.

FINISHED SIZE: Base, 15cm (6") square. Top
of trapezoid, 9cm ($3\frac{5}{8}$") square. Height, 4cm ($1\frac{5}{8}$").
MATERIALS: White heavy paper, 51cm by 36
cm ($20\frac{3}{8}$"×$14\frac{3}{8}$"). Stickers.

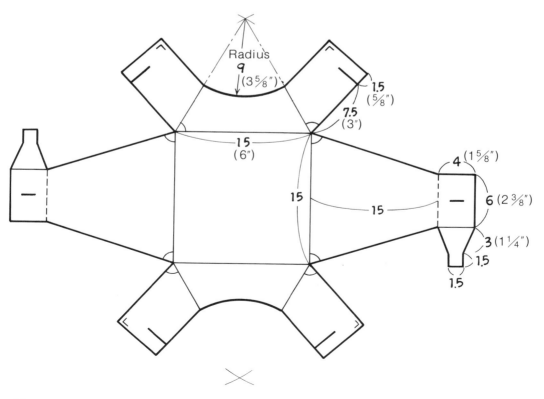

57 Triangular Pyramid,
shown on page 22.

FINISHED SIZE: One side of base, 8cm (3¼"). Height, 9cm (3⅝").
MATERIALS: Cobalt blue and light yellow heavy papers, 22cm by 15cm (8¾"×6") each. Stickers.

Use this lovely box for packing cookies or small cakes. Make in the same manner as box No. 25 shown on page 56, using the same pattern.

58 Paper Tote Bag,
shown on page 22.

Easy to make, it holds many things and is suitable for packing assorted gifts. Decorate the front and the back with stickers.

FINISHED SIZE: Length, 38cm (15¼"). Width, 38cm (15¼"). Depth, 15cm (6").
MATERIALS: Light blue heavy Japanese rice paper, 70cm by 46cm (28"×18⅜") for bag. Light blue heavy Japanese rice paper, 2 pieces of 20 cm by 13cm (8"×5¼") for handles. Stickers.

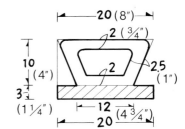

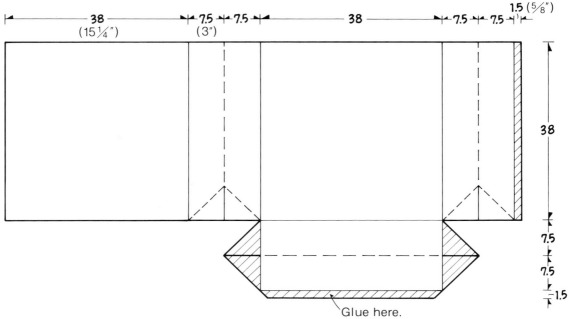

Glue here.

59 Rectangular Box, shown on page 23.

This is made of chic linen-mix paper. Note the manner of attaching ribbon. You can use this for keeping jewelry, too.

FINISHED SIZE: Length, 20cm (8"). Width, 8cm (3¼"). Height, 5.5cm (2¼").
MATERIALS: Dark brown heavy paper, 42cm by 30cm (16¾"×12") for inner box. Linen-mix paper, 36cm by 30cm (14⅜"×12") for lid. Dark red ribbon.

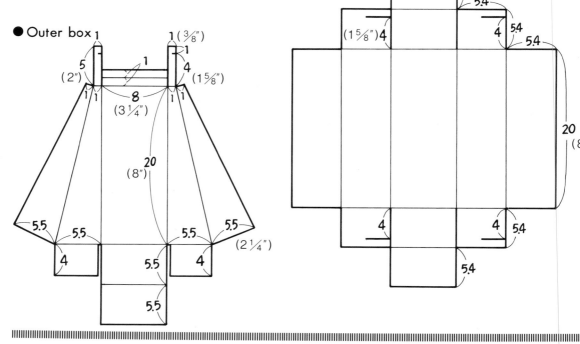

● Outer box

● Inner box

---

60 Square Box, shown on page 23.

Gift packages are a token of love, and make giver and recipient both happy. This box is made of red and green papers, but the pattern is the same as box No. 1 shown on page 36.

FINISHED SIZE: Length, 13cm (5¼"). Width, 13 cm (5¼"). Height, 13cm (5¼").
MATERIALS: Red and green Kent papers, 65cm by 65cm (26"×26"). Silver ribbon, 260cm (104").

Various Wrappings,
shown on pages 24 & 25.

Ribbons come in colors and materials to suit every package, from yarn, jute, or vinyl cord to prints, metallics, and tulle. Make the most of these great choices when you create your own distinctive gift packages.

Wrappings Nos. 62 - 71 shown on pages 24 and 25 are samples using ready-made gift boxes and handmade paper bags. Follow the instructions for these gift wraps and try making your own.

WRAP YOUR OWN:

We give gifts for special reasons or for no reason, for a wedding or birthday, or just because we've found something a friend would like. But in each instance we probably think more of our gift than of wrapping it beautifully, and the stores spoil us even more as each offers to wrap our selection for us. Then the giftwrap itself is so short-lived that we tend to take it for granted. But these are all good reasons to take the extra time to make a special, personalized giftwrap, for hostess gifts and weddings, so the person knows even more the thought we have put into finding something exactly right.

TYING THE RIBBON:

The bow is the decorative finale to your gift, so be sure you know how many goodlooking styles you have to choose from ! There are simple bows and star bows, pompons and tube and tucked bows. Review all the different materials and select the ribbons you want; then practice making great bows.

MATERIALS:

Select the wrapping paper and ribbons that are right for your gift. You can even use two different papers together. The range of choices is delightful prints, shiny or natural stocks, colorful cellophanes, crepe, and handmade rice paper, and all different thicknesses, too. And if you are wrapping an odd shape, use woodwool to fill the empty spaces. It now comes in so many colors. For wonderful finishing touches there are stickers and ribbons, and special sticker shapes you can cut yourself from purchased material.

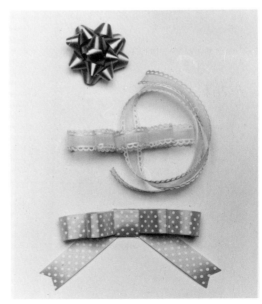

Slanting Rectangular Box, shown on page 26.

If you make gift boxes by yourself, you can create any shape you like. You will not need this shape often, but personalize it by adding colored paper or stickers over the surface.

FINISHED SIZE: Length, 6cm (2⅜"). Width, 6 cm (2⅜"). Height, 15cm (6").
Use any paper you like.

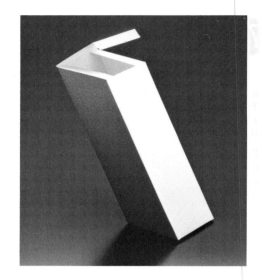

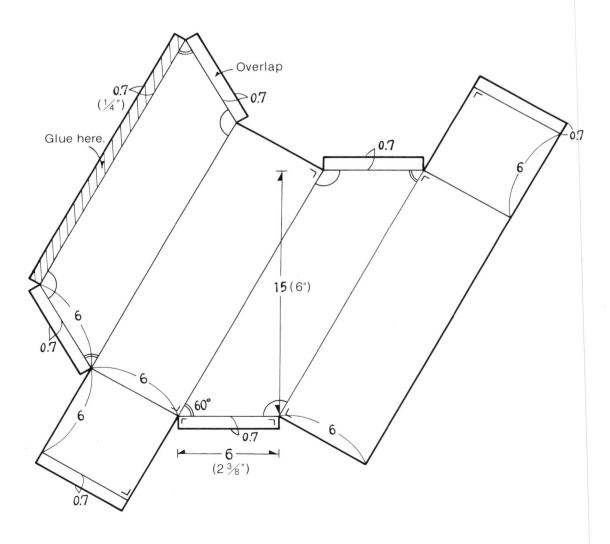

Overlap

0.7
(¼")

Glue here.

0.7

0.7

0.7

6

6

15 (6")

6

0.7

6

0.7

6

60°

0.7

6
(2⅜")

0.7

73 Trapezoid Box,
shown on page 26.

This can be used for an index case as well as a gift box. Heavy colored paper, heavy Japanese rice paper, or semi-transparent patterned paper will make an interesting box.

FINISHED SIZE: Base, 12cm (4¾") square. Height, 6cm(2⅜").
Use any paper you like.

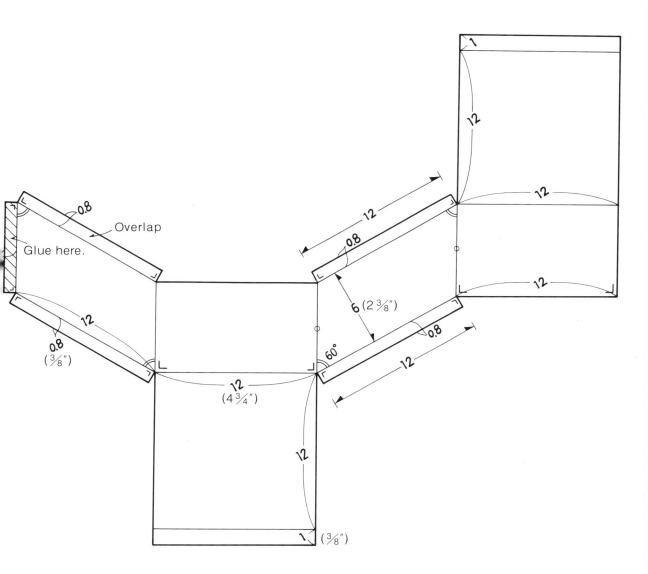

Overlap

Glue here.

0.8

0.8 (⅜")

12

12

12

12

12

6 (2⅜")

0.8

0.8

12

12

60°

12 (4¾")

12

1

1 (⅜")

Variation
of Triangular Pyramid,
shown on page 26.

This triangular pyramid has sharp ridges. It cannot be used as an all-purpose gift box, but can be an ornament or can be made into a vase for dried flowers by making a small hole at th the top. Try to make it from different kinds of paper.

FINISHED SIZE: See the pattern below.
Use any paper you like.

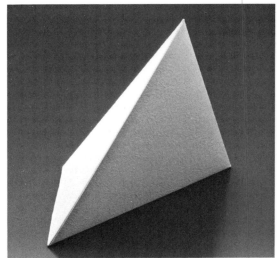

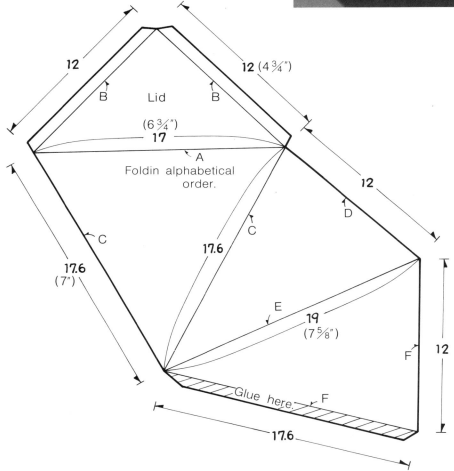

12

12 (4¾")

B   Lid   B

(6¾")
17
A
Foldin alphabetical
order.

12

C

D

17.6

C

17.6
(7")

E   19
(7⅝")

F

12

Glue here.   F

17.6

Tall Trapezoid Box,
shown on page 26.

This is a practical box for packing gifts, but the opening at the top is not big enough for a bulky object to go through. White embossed paper is used here.

FINISHED SIZE: Base, 10cm(4″)square. Height, 9.3cm (3¾″).
Use any paper you like.

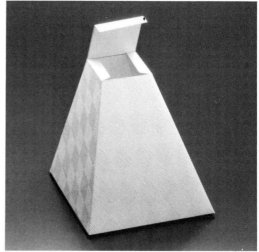

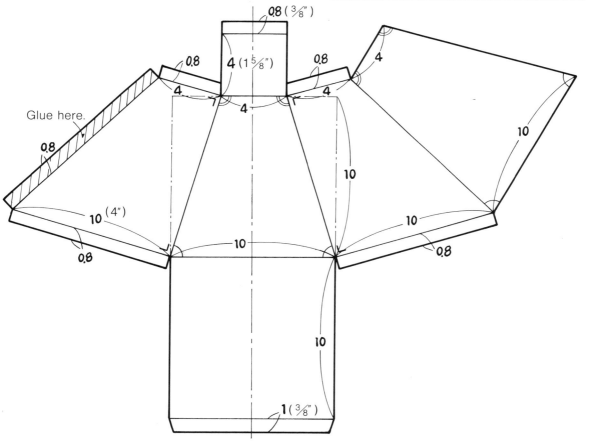